Lives of the Saints

Mary
with Prayers and Devotions

Edited by
Mark Etling

Regina
Press

Nihil Obstat: Reverend Robert O. Morrissey, J.C.D.
                 Censor librorum
                 May 14, 2004

Imprimatur: Most Reverend William Murphy
                Bishop of Rockville Centre
                June 7, 2004

THE REGINA PRESS
10 Hub Drive
Melville, New York 11747

Florentine Collection™, All rights reserved worldwide.
Imported exclusively by Malco.

Printed in U.S.A.

ISBN: 0-88271-759-6

Introduction

*T*he Virgin Mary is surely one of the most well-known and revered persons in the history of Christianity. She has been honored in prayer, art, music, and literature since the earliest days of the Catholic Church.

The reasons why she is so highly venerated are many.

First, the Blessed Mother is a model of Christian parenting. In raising the Christ Child, she exercised that delicate balance between assisting, guiding, and letting go that characterizes the very best of parents. And, of course, the most striking testimony to her abilities as a mother is found in the character of Jesus.

Second, Mary is an exemplar of the most noble of Christian virtues. Her patience in raising a Son who surely confused and bewildered her at times, her willingness to endure the suffering of witnessing Jesus' passion and death, and her faithful, unconditional love, all bear witness to her unfailing commitment to Christ.

Finally, Mary exemplifies the universal Christian call to holiness. Throughout her life, whatever the consequences, Mary remained always attentive and obedient to the will of God. She accepted in faith the call to be the Mother of the Savior. As the life of her Son Jesus mysteriously unfolded before her, she "treasured all these things and pondered them in her heart." And, even though her pain for her crucified Son must have been unbearable, she humbly and silently accepted the mysterious will of God for him.

Mary's greatness, and the heart of her mission on earth, are summed up in her words at the wedding feast of Cana: "Do whatever he tells you" (John 2:5). Every thought, feeling, and action in Mary's life pointed to Christ. It is the call of every Christian believer to do the same.

The Life of Mary

*T*he few available stories in the New Testament about Mary paint a picture of a simple and unassuming, yet strong and virtuous woman. What is most interesting is that the stories about her are never told in isolation. Her life is always connected in some way to her Son. In this regard, she serves as a role model for the Christian life, because the lives of believers are never solely their own. Their stories make sense only when connected to the life of Jesus.

Most of the details of Mary's life that are known to us are found in the Gospels. She was born in the town of Nazareth in Galilee, the daughter of Joachim and Anne. As a young woman, after having been betrothed to Joseph but not living together, the angel Gabriel announced to her that she would conceive and bear a son whose name would be Jesus. "He will be great and will be called Son of the Most High," Gabriel said (Luke 1:32). When Mary asked how she would conceive, since she was a virgin, the angel replied, "The holy Spirit will come upon you, and the power of the Most High will overshadow you. Therefore the child to be born will be called holy, the Son of God" (35). Mary's immediate response to the angel testifies to the depth of her trust in God: "Behold, I am the handmaid of the Lord. May it be done to me according to your word" (1:38).

The miraculous conception of Jesus led Joseph to believe he should divorce Mary quietly, in order to protect her from public humiliation. However, he was assured in a dream that the child had been conceived without the loss of virginity on the part of Mary, and so he took Mary into his home as his wife.

Mary then paid a visit to her cousin Elizabeth, who was pregnant with John the Baptist. As soon as she saw Mary, Elizabeth proclaimed, " Most blessed are you among women, and blessed is the fruit of your womb" (1:42). Mary responded with the beautiful hymn known as the Magnificat:

"My soul proclaims the greatness of the Lord;
    my spirit rejoices in God my savior.

For he has looked upon his
        handmaid's lowliness;
behold, from now on will all ages
        call me blessed.
The Mighty One has done great things for me,
        And holy is his name" (1:46-50).

As the time for Jesus' birth drew near, Joseph and Mary made their way to Bethlehem in order to participate in the census ordered by the Roman emperor Caesar Augustus. Because there was no room for them in the inn at Bethlehem, the couple had to stay in a stable. There the child Jesus was born. The Gospel tells us that Mary "wrapped him in swaddling clothes and laid him in a manger" (2:7).

Soon a group of shepherds came to pay homage to the newborn child after being told by an angel, "Today in the city of David a savior has been born for you" (2:11). Then, magi from the East came, bearing gifts for the child. The Gospel tells us that after these astonishing events took place, Mary "kept all these things, reflecting on them in her heart" (2:19).

But the inquiry of the magi aroused the suspicions of King Herod, who detested the thought of a rival to his throne. Herod ordered that all young male children in and around Bethlehem be slain, but Jesus was spared because an angel had warned Joseph to escape to Egypt with his wife and child. There they remained until Herod died.

At the appropriate time, the family came to the Temple to observe the rites of purification, as stipulated in the Law. While they were there, a man named Simeon took the child Jesus in his arms and spoke some troubling words to Mary: "Behold, this child is destined for the fall and the rising of many in Israel, and to be a sign that will be contradicted (and you yourself a sword will pierce) so that the thoughts of many hearts may be revealed" (2:34-35).

Mary gained even greater insight into the divinely appointed mission of her son after a Passover visit to Jerusalem. The twelve-year-old Jesus, without telling his parents, stayed behind in the city. After a frantic three-day search, Mary and Joseph found the boy in the Temple conversing with the learned teachers. Mary's concern and anxiety are reflected in her question to Jesus: "Son, why have you done this to us? Your father and I have been looking for you with great anxiety" (2:48). Jesus' reply was as perplexing to Mary as his disappearance had been: "Why were you looking for me? Did you not know that I must be in my Father's house" (2:49).

At this point, Mary recedes into the background of the Gospel narratives. Still, she makes an appearance on a few occasions. For example, she is present at the wedding feast of Cana, where Jesus performed his first miracle. On another occasion, Mary and some other relatives appear where Jesus is preaching, anxious to speak with him. On these occasions, Jesus reminds her and his followers that single-minded commitment to the Reign of God overrides all others, even the commitment to one's family.

In the Gospel of John, Mary, now apparently widowed, stands at the foot of the cross with the apostle John and some other women. As the final gesture of a loving son, Jesus directs John to take Mary into his home and care for her.

Mary's commitment to her Savior Son did not end with his death, resurrection, and ascension back to God. In the days before Pentecost she was present in the upper room with the apostles as they prayed for the coming of the Spirit.

Although not stated in the New Testament, Christian tradition holds that, because of her exemplary life and unique role as the Mother of God, Mary was assumed into heavenly glory at the end of her earthly life.

Devotion to Mary

*F*rom the earliest days of the Christian Church, devotion to Mary has had a special place in Christian spirituality. As early as the second century, the title "Mother of God" was given to Mary to emphasize the divinity of the Son she bore. In the fourth century, as a major controversy over the divine and human natures in Jesus was debated, Mary was given the title Theotokos ("God-bearer") to highlight the union of the human and divine in Jesus.

By the middle of the seventh century, the title "ever virgin" was ascribed to Mary to call attention to the belief that she remained a virgin throughout her life. Also at this time, the Church proclaimed the conviction that, because of her close and unique relationship with God, Mary was completely free from any taint of sin. This belief would eventually evolve into the doctrine of the Immaculate Conception, which holds that Mary was conceived without original sin.

Devotion to Mary grew dramatically during the Middle Ages. As the image of Christ as

Judge came to prominence in the Church at that time, Mary came to be understood more and more as the one who intercedes with her Son on behalf of sinners, the mediator of the mercy of Christ.

A visible symbol of Marian devotion is the worldwide proliferation of shrines in her honor. The basilica of St. Mary Major in Rome was built in the fourth century on the site where snow was miraculously supposed to have fallen in August. Mary has been venerated at the shrine of Montserrat in Spain since the twelfth century. Devotion to Our Lady of Czestochowa in Poland dates back to the fourteenth century. A major basilica in Mexico honors Our Lady of Guadalupe. Since the nineteenth century a number of Marian shrines have arisen, including Paris and Lourdes in France, Knock in Ireland, and Fátima in Portugal.

The Church celebrates several Marian feasts throughout the liturgical year:

The Solemnity of Mary, the Mother of God (January 1)

The Presentation of the Lord (February 2)

Our Lady of Lourdes (February 11)

The Annunciation (March 25)

The Immaculate Heart of Mary (Saturday after the second Sunday after Pentecost)

The Visitation (May 31)

Our Lady of Mount Carmel (July 16)

Dedication of the Basilica of St. Mary Major (August 5)

The Assumption (August 15)

The Queenship of Mary (August 22)

The Birth of Mary (September 8)

Our Lady of Sorrows (September 15)

Our Lady of the Rosary (October 7)

The Presentation of Mary (November 21)

The Immaculate Conception (December 8)

Our Lady of Guadalupe (December 12)

Prayers to Mary

Traditional Prayers

Sub Tuum Praesidium

(This prayer was first found in a Greek papyrus around A.D. 300. It is the oldest known prayer to the Virgin Mary.)

*W*e turn to you for protection,
holy Mother of God.
Listen to our prayers
and help us in our needs.
Save us from every danger,
glorious and blessed Virgin.

The Hail Mary

*H*ail, Mary, full of grace, the Lord is with thee. Blessed are thou among women, and blessed is the fruit of thy womb, Jesus. Holy Mary, Mother of God, pray for us sinners, now and at the hour of our death. Amen.

The Memorare

*R*emember, O most gracious Virgin Mary, that never was it known that anyone who fled to your protection, implored your help, or sought your intercession was left unaided. Inspired by this confidence I fly unto you, O virgin of virgins, my Mother. To you I come, before you I stand, sinful and sorrowful. O Mother of the Word Incarnate, despise not my petitions, but in your mercy, hear and answer me. Amen.

The Magnificat

*M*y soul proclaims the greatness of the Lord, my spirit rejoices in God my Savior for he has looked with favor on his lowly servant.

From this day all generations will call me blessed: the Almighty has done great things for me, and holy is his name.

He has mercy on those who fear him in every generation.

He has shown the strength of his arm,
he has scattered the proud in the conceit.

He has cast down the mighty from their thrones,
and has lifted up the lowly.

He has filled the hungry with good things,
and the rich he has sent empty away.

He has come to the help of his servant Israel
for he remembered his promise of mercy,
the promise he made to our fathers,
to Abraham and his children forever.

The Angelus

V. The angel of the Lord announced unto Mary,
R. And she conceived by the Holy Spirit.
Hail Mary . . .

V. "Behold the handmaid of the Lord . . .
R. "Be it done unto me according to your will."
Hail Mary . . .

V. And the Word became flesh . . .
R. And dwelt among us.
Hail Mary . . .

V. Pray for us, O holy Mother of God . . .
R. That we may be made worthy of the promises of Christ.

Let us pray. Lord, fill our hearts with your grace. Once, through the message of an angel you revealed to us the Incarnation of your Son; now, through his suffering and death lead us to the glory of his resurrection. We ask this through Christ our Lord. Amen.

Litany of the Blessed Virgin Mary

Lord, have mercy.
Christ, have mercy.
Lord, have mercy.
Christ, hear us.
Christ, graciously hear us.

God, the Father of heaven,

have mercy on us.
(Repeat "have mercy on us"
after each of the following intercessions.)
God the Son, Redeemer of the world,
God the Holy Spirit,
Holy Trinity, one God,

Holy Mary, pray for us.
(Repeat "pray for us"
after each of the following intercessions.)
Holy Mother of God,
Holy Virgin of virgins,
Mother of Christ,
Mother of the Church,
Mother of divine grace,
Mother most pure,
Mother most chaste,
Mother inviolate,
Mother undefiled,
Mother most amiable,
Mother most admirable,
Mother of good counsel,
Mother of our Creator,
Mother of our Savior,
Virgin most prudent,

Virgin most venerable,
Virgin most renowned,
Virgin most powerful,
Virgin most merciful,
Virgin most faithful,
Mirror of justice,
Seat of wisdom,
Cause of our joy,
Spiritual vessel,
Vessel of honor,
Singular vessel of devotion,
Mystical rose,
Tower of David,
Tower of ivory,
House of gold,
Ark of the covenant,
Gate of heaven,
Morning star,
Health of the sick,
Refuge of sinners,
Comforter of the afflicted,
Help of Christians,
Queen of angels,
Queen of patriarchs,
Queen of prophets,

Queen of apostles,
Queen of martyrs,
Queen of confessors,
Queen of virgins,
Queen of all saints,
Queen conceived without original sin,
Queen assumed into heaven,
Queen of the most holy rosary,
Queen of families,
Queen of peace,

Lamb of God,
   you take away the sins of the world;
Spare us, O Lord.
Lamb of God,
   you take away the sins of the world;
Graciously hear us, O Lord.
Lamb of God,
   you take away the sins of the world;
Have mercy on us.

Pray for us, O holy Mother of God.
That we may be made worthy of the
   promises of Christ.

Let us pray. O God, you willed that, at the message of an angel, your Word should take flesh in the womb of the Blessed Virgin Mary; grant to your suppliant people that we, who believe her to be truly the Mother of God, may be helped by her intercession with you. Through the same Christ our Lord. Amen.

Prayers of the Saints to Mary

Prayer of St. Francis of Assisi

*H*oly Virgin Mary, there is none like you among women born in the world. Daughter and handmaid of the heavenly Father, the almighty King, Mother of our most high Lord Jesus Christ, and spouse of the Holy Spirit, pray for us to your most holy Son, our Lord and Master.

Hail holy lady, most noble queen, Mother of God, and Mary ever virgin. You were chosen by the heavenly Father, who has been pleased to honor you with the presence of his most holy Son and the divine Paraclete.

You were blessed with the fullness of grace and goodness. Hail, Temple of God, his dwelling place, his masterpiece, his handmaid. Hail, Mother of God, I venerate you for the holy virtues that — through the grace and light of the Holy Spirit — you bring into the hearts of your devoted ones to change them from unfaithful Christians to faithful children of God. Amen.

Prayer of St. Anthony of Padua

Mary our Queen, holy Mother of God, we beg you to hear our prayer. Make our hearts overflow with divine grace and resplendent with heavenly wisdom. Render them strong with your might and rich in virtue. Pour down upon us the gift of mercy so that we may obtain the pardon of our sins. Help us to live in such a way as to merit the glory and bliss of heaven. May this be granted us by your Son Jesus, who has exalted you above the angels, and crowned you as Queen, and has seated you with him forever in his resplendent throne. Amen.

Prayer of St. Thomas Aquinas

Virgin full of goodness, Mother of mercy, I entrust to you my body and my soul, my thoughts and my actions, my life and my death. My Queen, come to my aid and deliver me from the snares of the devil. Obtain for me the grace of loving my Lord Jesus Christ, your Son, with a true and perfect love, and after him, O Mary, of loving you with all my heart and above all things. Amen.

Prayer of St. Francis de Sales

Most holy Mary Virgin Mother of God, I am unworthy to be your servant. Yet moved by your motherly care for me and longing to serve you, I choose you this day to be my queen, my advocate, and my mother. I firmly resolve ever to be devoted to you and to do what I can to encourage others to be devoted to you. My loving Mother, through the Precious Blood of your Son shed for me, I beg you to receive me as your servant forever. Aid me in my actions and beg for me the grace never by thought, word, or deed to be displeasing in your sight and that of your most holy Son. Remember me, dearest Mother, and do not abandon me at the hour of death. Amen.

Prayer of St. Alphonsus Liguori

O Mother of my God and my Lady Mary; as a beggar, all wounded and sore, presents himself before a great queen, so do I present myself before you, who are Queen of heaven and earth. From the lofty throne on which you sit, disdain not, I implore you, to cast your eyes on me, a poor sinner. God has made you so rich that you might assist the poor, and has made you Queen of Mercy in order that you might relieve the miserable. Behold me then, and pity me: behold me and abandon me not, until you see me changed from a sinner into a saint.

Prayer of St. Bernadette

*H*ow happy my soul was, good Mother, when I had the good fortune to gaze upon you! How I love to recall the pleasant moments spent under your gaze, so full of kindness and mercy for us. Yes, tender Mother, you stooped down to earth to appear to a mere child. . . . You, the Queen of heaven and earth, deigned to make use of the most fragile thing in the world's eyes. Amen.

Prayer of St. Thérèse of Lisieux

*V*irgin full of grace, I know that at Nazareth you lived modestly, without requesting anything more. Neither ecstasies, nor miracles, nor other extraordinary deeds enhanced your life, O Queen of the elect. The number of the lowly, "the little ones," is very great on earth. They can raise their eyes to you without any fear. You are the incomparable Mother who walks with them along the common way to guide them to heaven. Beloved Mother, in this harsh exile, I want to live always with you and follow you every day. I am enraptured by the contemplation of you and I discover the depths of the love of your heart. All my fears vanish under your motherly gaze, which teaches me to weep and to rejoice! Amen.

Prayer of Blessed Mother Teresa of Calcutta

Give us a heart as beautiful, pure, and spotless as yours. A heart like yours, so full of love and humility. May we be able to receive Jesus as the Bread of Life, to love him as you loved him, to serve him under the mistreated face of the poor. We ask this through Jesus Christ our Lord. Amen.

Prayers to Mary

Prayer of Our Lady of Lourdes

O Immaculate Virgin, mother of mercy, health of the sick, refuge of sinners, comforter of the afflicted, you know my wants, my troubles, my sufferings; look upon us in mercy.

By appearing in the Grotto of Lourdes to Saint Bernadette, you were pleased to make it a privileged sanctuary, whence you dispense your favors, and many have already obtained the cure of their infirmities, both spiritual and corporal. I come, therefore, with the most unbounded confidence to implore your maternal intercession.

Obtain for me, O loving Mother, what I request *(here mention your request)*. Through gratitude for your favors, I will endeavor to imitate your virtues, that I may one day share your glory.

Our Lady of Lourdes, Mother of Christ, you had influence with your divine Son while upon earth. You have the same influence now in heaven.

Pray for me; obtain for me from your divine Son my special request if it be divine will. Amen.

An Act of Consecration to
Our Lady of the Miraculous Medal

O Virgin Mother of God, Mary Immaculate, we dedicate and consecrate ourselves to you under the title of Our Lady of the Miraculous Medal.

May this medal be for each one of us a sure sign of your affection for us and a constant reminder of our duties toward you.

Ever while wearing it, may we be blessed by your loving protection and preserved in the grace of your Son.

O most powerful Virgin, Mother of our Savior, keep us close to you every moment of our lives.

Obtain for us, your children, the grace of a happy death; so that, in union with you, we may enjoy the bliss of heaven forever. Amen.

O Mary, conceived without sin, pray for us who have recourse to you.
(3 times)

Prayer to Our Lady of Knock

*O*ur Lady of Knock, Queen of Ireland, you gave hope to our people in a time of distress and comforted them in sorrow. You have inspired countless pilgrims to pray with confidence to your divine Son, remembering his promise: "Ask and you shall receive, seek and you shall find." Help me to remember that we are all pilgrims on the road to heaven. Fill me with love and concern for my brothers and sisters in Christ, especially those who live with me. Comfort me when I am sick or lonely or depressed. Teach me how to take part ever more reverently in the holy Mass. Pray for me now, and at the hour of my death. Amen.

Prayer to Our Lady of Guadalupe

*O*ur Lady of Guadalupe, mystical rose, make intercession for holy Church, protect the sovereign pontiff, help all those who invoke you in their necessities, and since you art the ever Virgin Mary and Mother of the true God, obtain for us from your most holy Son the grace of keeping our faith, sweet hope in the midst of the bitterness of life, burning charity and the precious gift of final perseverance.

Prayer to Our Lady of Czestochowa
(To be said each day upon arising)

*H*oly Mother of Czestochowa, you are full of grace, goodness and mercy. I consecrate to you all my thoughts, words and actions; especially my soul and body. I ask for your blessings and especially prayers for my salvation. Today, I dedicate myself to you, good Mother, totally; with my body and soul, amid joy and suffering, to obtain for myself and others your blessings on this earth and eternal life in heaven. Amen.

Prayer to Our Lady of Fátima

*M*ost Holy Virgin, who appeared at Fatima, to reveal to the three little shepherds the treasures of graces hidden in the recitation of the Rosary. Inspire our hearts with a sincere love of this devotion, in order that by meditating on the Mysteries of our Redemption that are recalled in it, we may gather the fruits and obtain the conversion of sinners, and *(here name the other favors you are praying for)*, which we ask of you in this Novena, for the greater glory of God, for your own honor, and for the good of souls. Amen.
Our Lady of the Rosary of Fatima, pray for us.

Prayer to Our Lady of Perpetual Help

*M*other of Perpetual Help, with greatest confidence I present myself to you. I implore your help in the problems of my daily life. Trials and sorrows often depress me; painful privations bring heartache into my life; often I meet the cross. Have pity on me, compassionate

Mother. Take care of my needs, free me from my sufferings or, if it be the will of God that I should suffer still longer, grant that I may endure all with love and patience. Mother of Perpetual Help, I ask this in your love and power.

Prayer to Our Lady of Mt. Carmel

Most beautiful flower of Mt. Carmel, fruitful vine, splendor of heaven, Mother of the Son of God and Immaculate Virgin, assist me in my hour of need. Star of the Sea, help me and show me that you are my mother.
Holy Mary, Mother of God, queen of heaven and earth, I humbly ask you from the bottom of my heart, to assist me in my hour of need. There are none that can withstand your power. Show me that you are my mother. Mary, conceived without sin, pray for us who have recourse to you.
(3 times)
Dear Mother, I place this cause in your hands.
(3 times)